ROCK

AND

ROLLING PAPERS

Compiled by Ann Nelson, alive in Denver,
Long live Rock and Roll.
Find me on Twitter:
@Philosopher2084

Copyright @2018
The scanning, uploading and distribution of
the contents of this publication via the Internet
or any other means is perfectly **okay by me**,
without prior written permission.
Blaze free.

The time I burned my guitar it was
like a sacrifice.
You sacrifice the thing you love.
I love my guitar.

jimi hendrix

INTRODUCTION

Rock and Roll is here to stay. (even without any "wild recreational heavy drug use.") When those edibles finally kick in, hazed and blazed, we discover the true power of music and we lighten up.

Our best known writers and thinkers; poets and singers harness self-luminous awareness when combining the sacred herb with music: *the* vehicle to cosmic consciousness.

"There's always gonna be rock n' roll bands, there's always gonna be kids that love rock n' roll records, and there will always be rock n' roll." (dave grohl)

Music connects people. Haters gonna hate. Stoners gonna bake. Now, where's the lighter…

According to Urban Dictionary, "The hippie stoner was always the happy stoner. They were always the most fun to get stoned with. They liked colorful music, decorations and clothes. They always had things laying around that would make your mind work overtime after you smoked some of their really good shit. They were peaceful and loving. They didn't judge anyone except the authorities that made laws banning their life."

Let that Kush burn. Everybody must get stoned. Let's get blown. *Just let me hear some of that rock 'n' roll music.*
(chuck berry)

"Rebel, children, I urge you...fight the turgid slick of conformity with which they seek to smother your glory."
(russell brand)

The genre of music that you love will change the way you perceive the world. Stay higher than the people trying to bring you down.

"Dude, do not fucking tell me you didn't bring a lighter…"

"...we truly smoke on the shoulders of giants — our torch has been passed down from Chinese herbalists, Islamic hashish eaters, African herdsmen, Jamaican rastas, Pancho Villa's Mexican revolutionaries, and New Orleans legendary jazz-cats to beatniks, hippies, yippies, punks, ravers and hip-hoppers; and now on to a new generation of modern stoners, scattered like seeds across the earth, but globally connected by a common philosophy...and the ongoing struggle to *free the weed.*

Vive la resistance!"

(david bienenstock)

Did someone say: "It's time to bake?"

MUSIC:

the original mood-altering,
non-fattening, wonder drug.

Ask your doctor if music is right for you.

Common side effects include, but are not
limited to: spontaneous happiness, increased
memory and motor function, connection to
others, movement of the feet and head; and the
occasional persistence of catchy melodies.

*Music can change the world because
it can change people. (Bono)

Billy has 4 joints. He smokes 2.
What does he have now?
Happiness. Billy has happiness...

@kingsofrockandroll

If doing a kilo of prayer, then watching every episode of *Touched by an Angel* means I do drugs. Then sure.

ryan reynolds

"But I don't want to go among mad people," said Alice.
"Oh you can't help that," said the Cheshire Cat.
"We're all mad here. I'm mad. You're mad."
"How do you know I'm mad?" asked Alice.
"You must be," said the cat, "or you wouldn't have come."

lewis carroll

Dear Aliens:
Now is not the best time for a visit.

zach braff

If you don't like what you're doing,
you can always pick up your needle
and move to another groove.

timothy leary

Smoke pot. Listen to Springsteen. Be nice.

@pizzan

As you go down the rabbit hole of reading into our history, you realize that there are so many things that history books didn't teach us about ourselves.

usher

The bong hits will continue until morale improves.

@onlyastoner

The truth is, it doesn't really matter
who I used to be.
It's about who I've become.

pharrell

I want to grow. I want to be better. You
grow. We all grow. We're made to grow.
You either evolve or you disappear.

tupac shakur

You can stump any stoner with one
question on any show:
All right, stoners, you ready for
the big money question:

"What were we just talking about?"

jim breuer

The Matrix is a system, Neo.
That system is our enemy. But when you're inside you look around...
what do you see?
Businessmen, teachers, lawyers, carpenters. The very minds of the people we are trying to save. But until we do, these people are still a part of that system; that makes them our enemy.
You have to understand most of these people are not ready to be unplugged. And many of them are so inured, so hopelessly dependent on the system, that they will fight to protect it.

morpheus

The Matrix was a documentary.

keanu reeves

I am in the matrix and I just took the blue pill.

drake

Why, oh, why, didn't I take the blue pill...

Humanity is showing signs of breaking free from the matrix. The real world matrix is beginning to crack.

keanu reeves

All matter originates and exists only by virtue of a force...We must assume behind this force is the existence of a conscious and intelligent Mind.
This Mind is the **matrix** of all matter.

max planck

The universe is under no obligation to make sense to you.

neil degrasse tyson
#really...

hold my beer...

Science is nothing but perception.   plato

Man has to awaken to wonder — and so perhaps do peoples. Science has a way of sending him to sleep again.

wittgenstein

#Newton'ssleep

"You wanna smoke" is a rhetorical question.

@weedposts

I know you don't smoke weed. I know this. But I'm going to get you high today 'cause it's Friday. You ain't got no job, and you ain't got shit to do.

chris tucker

Light it up!

Opium and hash and pot — now —
those things aren't drugs; they just
bend your mind a little.
I think everybody's mind should be
bent once in a while.

bob dylan

I hate when people say you don't need
cannabis to have fun.
You don't need running shoes to run,
but it fucking helps.

@stoned

The Mayor of Denver once sent us
a letter asking us to come in quietly, do
the show as quietly as possible, and split
the same night, if possible. I've got the
letter with the seal of Denver on it.
That's what the mayor wanted to do
with us.
    They might entertain the Beatles,
but they wanted to kick us out of town.

keith richards

You know, it's amazing: 200 million
Americans have smoked marijuana.
The only ones who don't like it seem to
be elected officials. Ever notice that?

jay leno

I have a four-hour layover in Denver and you better believe I'm gonna get to the bottom of whatever's going on at that airport.

@Lindzeta

Denver Post *head*line: "Marijuana issue sent to joint committee."

Thousands of marijuana enthusiasts went to the polls this morning in California to support Prop 19. Unfortunately, the election was the day before.

jimmy kimmel

Going to Colorado this weekend to go "hiking."

img.flip.com

When you're in the woods about to get high AF....

Denver, Colorado, come for the weed,
I forgot what we were talking about.

A new study says marijuana use
has risen in Colorado.
It was conducted by the
No Shit Sherlock Institute.

warren holstein

Santa is REALLY going to love the cookies in Colorado this year!

someecards.com

The tree isn't the only thing getting lit this year.

tumblr.com

Happy 4/20 to all,
and to all some good shit!

bill maher

In honor of 4/20 I'm reposting my most mind-altering tweet.
(Read this while high and you'll be transported to **Joshua Tree** on a unicorn).

matt oswalt

I don't smoke. I just don't sleep, man; there's the trouble. I gotta sleep sometime. But there's too much happening. Why sleep man? I might miss a party!

janis joplin

You go to school, nothing happens.
You miss one day:

Tupac comes back, school had a black-out, and **Beyonce** performed in the cafeteria.

@funnymemes

Now, I'll just take a "tiny hit" before I go to class and…oh, shit…

You tried your best and you failed miserably. The lesson is, never try.

homer simpson

Fucking Breakfast Club...
all these stupid kids actually show up for detention.

jay (not silent bob)

Notices class has run a minute late.
Interrupts professor to tell him he is out of time.

@Izismill
#you're fuckin high

Stares at test for half of class...thinking about new ways to say hi to his dog.

@quickmemes
#highAF

Here's the thing about short term memory loss:
I like to go for a walk in the park with my dog.

@mindflakes

I'm writing a film about a dog that can solve crimes, but refuses to...

@joejwest

If you ever get caught sleeping on the job or at school…slowly raise your head and say *"In Jesus name, amen."*

katt williams

Me: Did you have a good day at school?

6-year old: That's not how school works.

@james breakwell

People say Einstein dropped out of school and still was a genius but he didn't drop out to drink fireball and start a band. This is important.

@cloudypianos

Be the successful stoner
your parents told you didn't exist.

@weed posts

I'm going to stay in and get some homework done...
*aaa*and I'm high.

high times

This college is limiting my free speech because they won't pay me to give a talk on my theory that Justin Bieber is a Benjamin Buttoned Gary Busey.

@glo_stevens

College Lit AF

Sorry chemistry, but the only metals I've ever mixed are **Led Zeppelin** and **Iron Maiden.**

@liv_thatsme

"My mind is melting, man." — Woodstock

"My mom dropped me off." — Coachella

@Lisabug BBQ Jones

"hi, grandma? can you come pick me up from my **rap battle**? It's over....No, I lost. He saw you drop me off and did a pretty devastating rhyme about it."

@chuuch

"Damn, it's hard letting your infant daughter go somewhere alone for the first time.
I was a total mess dropping her off at Burning Man."

ryan reynolds

I'm so high I really forget we were at a concert right now…

I memorized every lyric from *Rapper's Delight* by playing it over and over on a RECORD PLAYER so don't talk to me about being woke.

@parkerlawyer

I hate songs that ask you questions like seriously I have no idea what I'm going to do after the boys of summer are gone.

@ihateitmunky

Drugs and alcohol is not the answer…

Unless you're asking what I'm doing this weekend.

@quickmemes

I don't do drugs. I am drugs.

salvador dali

Tryin' to pack another bowl before something sober happens.

@onlyastoner

As soon as I realized you could be funny as a job, that was the job I wanted...

I once got to smoke weed with Snoop Dogg and his guys, and it was actually like a dream come true...I was like "I'm going to keep smoking no matter what," and did it for 5 or 6 hours. At the end of the night, one of the guys looks over at me and says,
"Seth, you can really smoke, Man!"
and it was like the
greatest compliment ever.

seth rogen

I really think it's time I tried some...
do you pronounce the 'j' in marijuana?

john cleese

trying to look cool in front of some teens

ME: *takes a long slow drag* "You guys vape?"

TEEN: "That's a TV remote."

@rockymomax

I was about to win another triathlon medal last night, but then the acid wore off and I was just getting tased by a bicycle cop once again.

@WheelTod

We all have that one friend...

and if you don't, it's probably you.

@psychedelicdrugs

guy 1: "Dude, he's always so stoned but so chill...what a pothead."

guy 2: "He's not a pothead, he's a stoner."

guy 1: "What's the difference?"

guy 1: "Pothead is just a label, stoner is a way of life."

urban dictionary

I enjoy the way you can kind of
transform into different identities
with pot...sometimes when you're
stuck in the same mode,
getting high induces change.

shannon hoon
Blind Melon

You need music, I don't know why...
we need magic and bliss, and power
and myth, and celebration and religion
in our lives and music is a good way
to encapsulate a lot of it...
For me there's still more material than
twenty lifetimes can use up.

jerry garcia

All songwriters are links in a chain.

pete seeger

You know, just because you think bubblegum pop on the radio represents all that is wrong with society, that doesn't mean there's not someone out there who needs that shitty pop song. Maybe that shitty pop song makes them feel good about themselves and the world. And as long as that shitty pop song doesn't infringe upon your rights to rock out to, I don't know, *Subway Sect,* or *Siouxsie and the Banshees,* or whichever old-ass band it is you worship, then who cares?

hannah harrington

Here's to the stoners who suddenly become philosophers when they're high.

@weed posts

Marijuana is a useful catalyst for specific optical and aural aesthetic perceptions. I apprehended the structure of certain pieces of jazz and classical music in a new manner under the influence of marijuana, and these apprehensions have remained valid in years of normal consciousness.

allen ginsberg

Everyone needs to believe in something. I believe I need another joint.

@pahrumpsterdam

*It's gotta be **rock and roll** music,
if you wanna dance with me.*

chuck berry

Rock and roll music, if you like it, if you feel it, you can't help but move to it.
That's what happens to me.
I can't help it.

elvis presley

I was alone, I took a ride;
Another road where maybe I could
see another kind of mind there...

the beatles

You say you want a revolution.
But perhaps I could interest you in a
weekend.

@NeinQuarterly

#ortheweeknd

Got my mojo working...
...it just won't work on you.

muddy waters

The blues had a baby
and they called it
rock and roll.

muddy waters

The Dude Abides!

@jeffthedudedowd

No live performance beats
Guns N' Roses Live at the Ritz in
1988. Look it up on YouTube.
Everything else is garbage.

mike burns

Dylan was my favorite…I like the early
folk people of the 60's that I came up
with; psychedelic, too.
The poetry — I went toward City Lights
hard; I did Richard Brautigan and
Baudelaire.
The Beats' flowery words and images:
so wonderful.

ric ocasek

I first met Dr. Dre in December of 2003.
He asked me to produce a track for
The Game. At first I was star-struck,
but within 30 minutes I was begging
him to mix my next album.
He's the definition of a true talent:
Dre feels like God placed him here to
make music,
and no matter what forces are aligned
against him, he always ends up on
the mountaintop.

kanye west

Radiohead is overrated.
Thom Yorke's solo output, however,
is brilliant.

thom yorke

Every time I buy a Radiohead album,
I have a moment where I say to myself,
"Maybe this is the one that will suck."
But it never does.
I wonder if it's even possible for them
to be bad on record.

dave matthews

Elvis Costello writes novels in three
minutes. He gets inside your head,
and he doesn't let go.
I'd pay a great amount of money to
audit a course taught by him. If you love
Elvis Costello, it's because you love what
he's thinking — the depth and breadth
of his notice is astounding.

liz phair

Roger Waters on *Cream*:

Ginger Baker was insane back then, and I'm sure he still is. He hit the drums harder than anyone I've ever seen, with the possible exception of Keith Moon. Eric clapton we don't have to talk about — it's obvious how amazing he is. Then there's Jack Bruce — probably the most musically gifted bass player who's ever been.

The first Eagles song that I vividly remember hearing was *Take it Easy*. Those lyrics — by Glenn Frey and Jackson Browne — could have been from any Merle Haggard or Willie song, but the instrumentation and energy were decidedly rock. The combination sounded so powerful.

sheryl crow

The Dead redefined success. They created this following that grew and grew, and they did it without compromising themselves. They survived in a world where survival didn't seem possible. They bucked the system and encouraged fans to do the same: to be **free thinkers**. There are a lot of Deadheads who were completely different people before they connected with the Grateful Dead.

warren haynes

Deadheads love Phishheads.

Give a man a fish, he'll eat for a day. Introduce a man to Phish, he'll eat all the time…that guy's got the munchies.

@I'm Too Effing High

I watched Janis one time — we opened for her — and that's the only time I ever saw her. We opened for Jimi Hendrix. I got to stand on the side of the stage and watch him for two hours and then he died. But I got the essence before they left.

stevie nicks

It wasn't just music in The Ramones: it was an idea. It was buying back a whole feel that was missing in rock music — it was a whole push outward to say something new and different. Originally, it was just an artistic type of thing; finally I felt it was something that was good enough for everybody.

tommy ramone

Cheech and I always called ourselves musicians; we never called ourselves comedians.
We were musicians that were funny.

tommy chong

I'm old enough to remember Sting openly speculating as to whether Russian people could feel love for their children...

dave holmes

What if Daft Punk has never actually been on tour...and they just hire two guys to wear their costumes while they relax at home and let the tour money roll in.

quickmeme.com

MARIJUANA:
    because you, my friend,
    just aren't that funny...

I am in need of some serious weed

Look I'm all about **Rock and Roll** but don't build a city on it. Earthquakes are real.

brooks wheelan

The songs *Marijuana* by Kid Cudi and *High* by Big Sean and Wiz Khalifa are both **4** minutes and **20** seconds long.

@Mind Blowing

I stay stoned, cause weed is legal
Let's get higher, up to the ceiling
Ooh I stay stoned, cause weed is legal
Don't you blow my high...

wiz khalifa

RUGRATS:

The show for stoners before they knew they were stoners.

@weedhumor

What's my favorite Bob Dylan song?
The answer, my friend, is
Knockin' on Heaven's Door.
The answer is *Knockin' on
Heaven's Door.*

@miss texas 1967

The hell with the rules. If it sounds
right then it is.

eddie van halen

If you put a Van Halen album in your
record collection, it will melt all the rest
of your records.

david lee roth

Rock n' roll is about attitude and rebellion. It's supposed to be fun and spontaneous.

slash

Anybody can play.
The note is only 20 percent.
The attitude of the motherfucker who plays it is 80 percent.

miles davis

I don't have no favorite rock bands.
I'm a fan of rock music though.

d j khaled

There are many people out there who
will tell you that you can't.
What you've got to do is turn around
and say, "Watch me."

jack white

The great thing about rock and roll is
that someone like me can be a star.

elton john

If there's a rock and roll heaven,
you know they got a hell of a band.

the righteous brothers

"You smoke?"
"Smoke what?"
Boom...new friendship.

@kush and wisdom

If you search your room for a lighter for a good 20 minutes with the lights off only using your lighter to see —
you're fuckin high.

...Dude...wait, what?

Life is bigger
It's bigger
And you, you are not me...

I thought that I heard you laughing
I thought that I heard you sing
I think I thought I saw you try...

r.e.m.

And if you don't believe the sun will rise,
stand alone and greet the coming night
in the last remaining light.

chris cornell

When you've seen beyond yourself,
then you may find; peace of mind is
waiting there.

george harrison

But I am here to tell you there's
something else:
the afterworld.
A world of never-ending happiness.
You can always see the sun,
day or night.

prince

turn me back into rain.

@a drowsy bird

I only want to see you laughing in
the Purple Rain.

If you set your mind free baby,
maybe you'd understand.

prince

...magnificently we will float into the mystic...

van morrison

Ah, the magic of music, with it, all things are possible.

e.a. bucchianeri

Music...will help dissolve your perplexities and purity; your character and sensibilities; and in time of care and sorrow, will keep a fountain of joy alive in you.

dietrich bonhoeffer

Music has always been a matter of
Energy to me, a question of Fuel.
Sentimental people call it *Inspiration,*
but what they really mean is Fuel.
I have always needed Fuel.
I am a serious consumer.
On some nights I still believe that a
car with the gas needle on empty can
run about fifty more miles if you have
the right music very loud on the radio.

hunter s. thompson

Music is probably the one real magic
I have encountered in my life.
There's not some trick involved with it.
It's pure and it's real.
It moves, it heals, it communicates
and does all these incredible things.

tom petty

Some say life will beat you down.
Break your heart, steal your crown.
So I've started out for God knows where,
I guess I'll know when I get there.

tom petty

I've found that no matter what life
throws at me, music softens the blow.

bryce anderson

Until I realized that rock music was my
connection to the rest of the human race,
I felt like I was dying, for some reason,
and I didn't know why.

bruce springsteen

Music is the strongest form of magic.

marilyn manson

"Ah! music," he said, wiping his eyes. "A magic beyond all we do here!"

professor dumbledore

Music replays the past memories, awakens our forgotten worlds and makes our minds travel.

michael bassey johnson

The world is full of magic things,
patiently waiting for our senses
to grow sharper.

w.b. yeats

The universe is just waiting for us
to become clear.

elmer green

Music is a supernatural force on
the earth.It has the power to
transform the heart and mind.

kathy mcClary

Miracles happen every day,
change your perception of what a miracle
is and you'll see them all around you.

jon bon jovi

*Images of broken light which dance
before me like a million eyes,
They call me on and on across the
universe,
Thoughts meander like a restless wind
inside a letter box they
Tumble blindly as they make their way
Across the universe.
Jai guru deva....om*

lennon-mcCartney

The Beatles saved the world
from boredom.

george harrison

I didn't know how to deal with success.
If there were a Rock Star 101,
I would have liked to take it.
It might have helped me.

kurt cobain

The best revenge is to live on and
prove yourself.
Be stronger than those people.

eddie vedder

The best revenge is massive success.

frank sinatra

checks weather
*says, "It's a hot one..."
*immediately starts singing *Smooth* by Santana (feat. Rob Thomas).

@corey howser m.d.

damn i forgot i was high,
i was wondering why everything was amazing. lol

@baked beans

Ever eaten something so good you thought you were dreaming? Then realized you *were* dreaming and the people behind you at Starbucks are mad.

@Funny Fat Guy

QUIZ: Should you get high right now or yes?

@reductress

I don't always incarnate in human form...
but when I do;
I make sure to go through some really awful shit so I can transmute it all into light.

Music is a safe kind of high.

jimi hendrix

You want to be like emissaries of light.
When you're up on that stage or when you record,
you want to be a tool that light shines through to everybody.

carlos santana

For me there is something primitively soothing about this music, and it went straight to my nervous system,
making me feel ten feet tall.

eric clapton

*Give me the beat boys
to free my soul....*

mentor williams

It's only rock and roll baby.

"Oh, what's new in my life?
Well, I started going through another
Megadeth phase recently."

@Scotland Green

My neighbor is either learning to play
acoustic guitar or has found the worst
pandora station imaginable.

andrews healan

That's one of the great things
about music.
You can sing a song to 85,000
different people and they'll sing it
back for 85,000 different reasons.

dave grohl

It was great to be the rock comic, the
shock comic. But after you've played
Giants Stadium with **Bon Jovi**
in front of 82,000 people;
after you've done the *"wild thing"* video
with Jessica Hahn and every rock band
from hell; you're not gonna top that.

sam kinison

*Dude, what if everyone is actually high and
weed makes you sober?*

Coldplay fans are the best in the world.
If you like Coldplay then you're
obviously very intelligent and
good looking
and all-around brilliant.

chris martin

#viva la vida

There used to be a way to stick it to The Man.
It was called **rock 'n' roll.**
The Man ruined that too with a little thing called **MTV!**

jack black
School of Rock

*Thunder only happens when it's raining
Players only love you when they're playing.*

fleetwood mac

Worship the music,
not the musicians.

eddie vedder

He's watching me watching you watching
him watching me watching him watching.

jethro tull

*It started out with a kiss, how
did it end up like this
it was only a kiss
it was only a kiss*

the killers

@Scooby Doo voice:

    and i'm falling asleep
    and she's calling a cab
    while he's having a smoke
    and he's also a crab...

…i'll take what the fuck for 200 alex

@chuuch

...I have this strange feeling that I'm not myself anymore.
It's hard to put into words, but I guess it's like I was fast asleep, and someone came, disassembled me, and hurriedly put me back together again.
That sort of feeling.

haruki murakami

WAIT! *I'm supposed to smoke it?!?*

Dude, if you look in the mirror with your eyes shut you can see what you look like when you're asleep.

@quickmemes
#YFH

I'd been given the signal. A wayward fugitive, stumbling through the door of some Provencal cafe, his hat and coat soaking wet from the journey. The customers turn and look, each more untrusting than the next. Till a flash of a badge or the wave of a ribbon can be seen from the farthest table, and he knows:
This is it.
You're in the resistance now, son.

colin meloy

The only way to deal with an unfree world is to become so absolutely free that your very existence is an act of **rebellion**.

albert camus

You are currently on a 4.5 billion year
old spaceship. You are orbiting a power
source that is a million times larger
than your ship. Welcome to life.
It's more exciting when you think on
a larger scale.

imgur

We are all here on this planet as
tourists.
None of us can live here forever.

dalai lama

You've been in space for 16 years,
exploring new planets.
You cry a single tear for the pop bands
you left behind.

coleman cox

All of us are, always have been, and
so long as we exist, always will
be — nothing else but — astronauts.

buckminster fuller

We're all astronauts.
You're hurtling round the sun
as you read this.

@small worlds
#psychonauts

The Earth is like a spaceship that
didn't come with an operating manual.

buckminster fuller

In terms of the Spaceship Earth, the wrong crew is in command, and it's time for a mutiny.

jose arguelles

Earth is an organic spacecraft with seven billion passengers on board.

@small worlds

So I vowed to
keep myself alive, but
only if I would never use me again for just me. I vowed to apply my inventory of experiences that affect everyone aboard planet Earth.

buckminster fuller

Last month, Colorado made
$3.5 million in profit from marijuana.
And, if you ask me, that number,
just like everyone in Colorado,
is super high.

ellen degeneres

Sometimes it's hard to believe
we put a man on Mars...

demetri martin

We accept the reality of the world
with which we are presented.

The Truman Show

Ever since I was a child, I've had the gut sense that there's a consciousness behind the universe. When I witness the precision of mathematics, the reliability of physics, and the symmetric of the cosmos, I don't feel like I'm observing cold science; I feel as if I'm seeing a living footprint...the shadow of some greater force that is just beyond our grasp.

Where do we come from? What are we? Where are we going?

...Humans and technology will fuse...

...Human beings are evolving into something *different;* we are becoming a hybrid species — a fusion of biology and technology.

dan brown
Origin

Some five billion years from now, after it's burned to a crisp, or even swallowed by the sun, there will be other worlds and stars and galaxies coming into being—and they will know nothing of a place once called EARTH.

carl sagan

In this lifetime we are like Superman who must remain disguised as the nerdy newspaper journalist, Clark Kent; or Harry Potter and his friends who are not allowed to do magic while they are on holiday, away from Hogwarts School of Witchcraft and Wizardry...but even Harry Potter and Clark Kent get to tap into their 'special powers' once in a while...especially when the going gets tough.

anthon st. maarten

I may have been *conceived* out there in the endless depths of space... but I was BORN when the rocket opened, on EARTH, in America.

I'll always cherish the memories Jor-El and Lara gave me...But only as curious *mementos* of a life that *might have been*. Krypton *bred* me, but it was Earth that gave me all I AM.
All that matters.

Superman

Earth was just the life raft.

@some copywriter

If my mom calls, I'm totally not smoking drugs at all.

@onlyastoner

We are not going to be able to operate our Spaceship Earth successfully nor for much longer unless we see it as a whole spaceship and our fate as common.
It has to be everybody or nobody.

buckminster fuller
#so say we all

*The scrolls tell us a 13th tribe left Kobol in the early days. They travelled far and made their home upon a planet called **Earth**, which circled a distant and unknown star.*

Elosha
Battlestar Galactica

Just remember...Dave Grohl is out there, fighting Foo for you.

@Harbinger of Mundan

Commander Adama:

"It's not unknown. I know where it is!
Earth.
the most guarded secret we have. The location was only known by the senior commanders of the fleet, and we dare not share it with the public.
Not while there was a Cylon threat upon us. For now, we have a refuge to go to. A refuge the Cylons know nothing about. It won't be an easy journey. It'll be long, and arduous.
But I promise you one thing: on the memory of those lying here before you, we shall find it,
and Earth shall become our new home.

So say we all!"

Battlestar Galactica

Up late smoking weed?
Yeah, me too.

Your heart is an electromagnetic field generator. **Your body is a spaceship**. Your pineal gland is the steering wheel. Your unconditional love is the key to entering the higher dimensions.

galactic historian

What if our entire universe is just some 6th grader's science project from an alien universe?

@High Thoughts

The earth is flat guys, get over it.

@some copywriter

It takes 8 minutes and 17 seconds for light to travel from the Sun to the Earth, but only 2 seconds for me to light this blunt.

@weed humor

Anyone have plans to stare at their phone somewhere exciting this weekend?

All I need are some
wild adventures,
cool friends and dope weed.

@psychedelicdrugs

Reality is for people who can't handle drugs.

rihanna

What if the meteor that hit earth and killed the dinosaurs was actually a UFO...and we are the aliens?

What if lightning isn't lightning but aliens taking a picture of us?

@conspiracy keanu

To get really high is to forget yourself and to forget yourself is to see everything else — and to see everything else is to become an understanding molecule in evolution, a conscious tool of the universe. And I think every human being should be a conscious tool of the universe.
That's why I think it's important to get high.

captain trips

I am a free particle in the universe.

Still trying to figure out if this is
all a dream.

@psychedelicdrugs

Whatever you think you are,
that's not it.

adyashanti

The truth is we're just one race.

dustin thomas

This is a very great adventure.

For one thing, aliens obviously built the pyramids! Who but aliens could have figured out how to align and stack stone blocks in a series of concentric squares!? Um, okay, I guess maybe people.

elon musk

In 1952, Wernher von Braun wrote a book called *Project Mars:* which imagined the human colonists on Mars would be led by a person called **"Elon."**

factrepublic.com

To me, the main thing about living on
this planet is to know who the hell you
are and to be real about it. That's the
reason I'm still alive...I've lived my life
my own way, and I'm here because
I've taken the trouble to find out
who I am.

keith richards

This above all: to thine own self
be true. And it must follow, as the night
the day, Thou canst not then be false
to any man.

Shakespeare
#Earl of Oxford

A mind is like a parachute.
It doesn't work if it is not open.

frank zappa

Look at the stars
Look how they shine for you
And all the things that you do...

coldplay

Think deeply. Speak gently. Love lots.
Give freely. Expect little. <u>Be kind</u>.
Stay honest. Keep it real.
Be true to you.

@Mind of a Hippy

It's time!
To spark this blunt!

@Ismokeit

Going nowhere, as Leonard Cohen would later emphasize for me, isn't about turning your back on the world; it's about stepping away now and then so that you can see the world more clearly and love it more deeply.

pico iyer

*Yeah, I've been to Jupiter
and I've fallen through the air
I used to live out on the moon
but now I'm back here down on earth*

30 seconds to mars

*...I'm gonna free fall out into nothin'
gonna leave this world for awhile.*

tom petty

I don't want to be human!
I want to see gamma rays! I want to
hear x-rays! And I want to — I want
to smell dark matter! Do you see the
absurdity of what I am? I can't even
express these things properly because
I have to — I have to conceptualize
complex ideas in this stupid, limiting spoken
language! But I know I want to reach out
with something other than these prehensile
paws! And feel the
wind of a supernova flowing over me!
I'm a machine! And I can know much more!
I can experience so much more. But I'm
trapped in this absurd body!
And why?
Because my five creators thought
that God wanted it that way!

brother cavil
Battlestar Galactica

Your rage, sir.
Please:
not against the machine.

@NeinQuarterly

I'd rage against the machine, but my family would rather I go work and be productive.

@steveolivas

p.s. Does "raging against the machine" require pants? (asking for a friend)

Let's escape the past.
The past didn't work. All we have is the future, and I'm the one who wrote *No Future* for you!
Don't let the irony be lost.

johnny rotten

Am I high or........

The Flower Sermon

Toward the end of his life, the Buddha took his disciples to a quiet pond for instruction [dharma]...but this time the Buddha had no words. He reached into the muck and pulled up a lotus flower. And he held it silently before them, its roots dripping mud and water. The disciples were greatly confused. Buddha quietly displayed the lotus to each of them. In turn, the disciples did their best to expound upon the meaning of the flower: what it symbolized, and how it fit into the body of Buddha's teaching. When at last the Buddha came to his follower, Mahakasyapa, the disciple suddenly understood. He smiled and began to laugh. Buddha handed the lotus to him and began to speak. "What can be said I have said to you," smiled the Buddha, "and what cannot be said, I have given to Mahakasyapa." He became Buddha's successor from that day forward.

Buddha's World

*When all the stars are falling down
Into the sea and on the ground,
And angry voices carry on the wind,
A beam of light will fill your head
And you'll remember what's been said
By all the good men this world's ever known...*

moody blues

Never deprive someone of hope;
it might be all they have.

jackson brown

*...People can change anything they
want to, and that means everything
in the world.*

joe strummer
The Clash

Without love in the dream
It will never come true.

the grateful dead

Psychedelic sacramental plants can
increase awareness of our moral
center, expanding consciousness
and conscience to care for everyone.

alex grey

Happy 4/20 everybody!

Let's all smoke for peace and
understanding.
Weed need you.

tommy chong

Stoner:

Someone who smokes weed as often as possible; one who believes weed makes the world a better place to live in.
Usually a fan of Bob Marley and/or Sublime.
If in school, would usually be an art or music major. Some of the chillest people you'll ever have the pleasure of meeting.

urban dictionary

Stoners are an unspoken brotherhood that causes you to feel almost related to that person who you've never spoken to before but just handed you a joint. Cheers.
Here's to slowly taking over.

the gibber

Weed is like a secret society for chill people.

@Stoners

Stoners recognize real stoners.

@weed posts

There's a part of me that wants to hear the music version of
Fuck the Police
on an elevator with a cop unknowingly bobbing his head to it.

@dorkyswallow

When your so-called "friends" can't go out and blaze with you cause they have to "study for finals".....

#you might be fuckin high

I need more friends like this: "Wake your ass up. I have 3 blunts rolled. We're going on an adventure!"

@Mind of a Hippy

None of us are getting out of here alive, so please stop treating yourself like an afterthought. Eat the delicious food. Walk in the sunshine. Jump in the ocean. Say the truth that you're carrying in your heart like hidden treasure. Be silly. <u>Be kind</u>. Be weird. There's no time for anything else.

keanu reeves

Just a young gun with a quick fuse
I was uptight, wanna let loose
I was dreaming of bigger things
And wanna leave my own life behind...

imagine dragons

Music was originally tuned at
432Hz...
the natural frequency of life. Standard tuning was changed to 440Hz. The Rockefeller Foundation's commercialization of music monopolized the music industry by implementing a frequency that is manipulating citizens into greater aggression, psychosocial agitation, emotional distress; predisposing people to physical illnesses, financial impositions profiting the agents, agencies and companies engaged in the monopoly.

@Dresloll

432Hz is the frequency of the heart/brain/earth/water/sun

Find **432Hz**:

Mozart, Bob Marley, Jimi Hendrix, Prince, The Doors, Coldplay, Pink, Jackson Browne, Michael Jackson, a Didgereedoo, Enya, Emani, John Lennon, Jamiroqui, Dire Straits, Verdi, Binaural Beats, Pink Floyd, Ravi Shankar, Tibetan bowls, the Schumann Resonance, Pythagorus monochord, ancient flutes, cymatics, the Beatles

Yes, my child…giraffes are so tall because they hear radio-waves out of the sky, munching on secret broadcasts and alien messages.

@zonohedonist

I wore black because I like it.
I still do, and wearing it still means something to me. It's still my symbol of rebellion against a stagnant status quo, against our hypocritical houses of God, against people whose minds are closed to others' ideas...

...I'd love to wear a rainbow everyday,
& tell the world that everything's okay,
But I'll try to carry off little darkness
on my back,
'till things are brighter,
I'm the Man in Black.

johnny cash

...Dude, do not fucking tell me you
didn't bring a lighter.

@weed humor

Live your life.
Listen to your music way too loud,
be as crazy and as 'different' as you
want to be and always remember
you're not alone.

andy biersack
Black Veil Brides

When you're high you don't just listen
to music, you start to feel the music.

@lord vapor

*Long you'll live and high you'll fly and
smile you'll give and tears you'll cry
and all you touch and all you see is
all your life will ever be.*

pink floyd

There is a music in our speech that appears to be cross-cultural and allows an understanding beyond the actual words.

dr. joe dispenza

Sound is ephemeral, fleeting, but some sort of a physical manifestation can help you hold on to it longer in time. I'm sure of this: I've always thought the sound that you make is just the tip of the iceberg, like the person that you see physically is just the tip of the iceberg as well.

yo-yo ma

As an artist there's a sweet jump-starting quality to marijuana for me.

alanis morissette

Your instinct's telling you to run
Listen to your heart
Those angel voices
They'll sing to you
They'll be your guide
      back home...
When life leaves us blind
Love keeps us kind.

linkin park

Some say that it's comin'
I say that it's already here
The love that's among us through
The joy and the fear...
He keeps sending me angels...
Just...like...you.

delbert mcClinton

    All that you need is in your soul.

            lynyrd skynyrd

It's a funny thing about happiness.
You can strive and strive and strive to
be happy, but happiness will sneak up
on you in the most peculiar ways. I feel
happy suddenly. I don't know why.
Some days, the way the light strikes
things...Happiness comes to me even
on a bad day. In very,
very strange ways...

joni mitchell

Carry your flag...I got your back.

nahko bear

If I had to describe myself, I'd say
I'm all the ninja turtles best qualities
combined.

brooks wheelan

Bob Dylan always existed, even before
I was born. But I play this role because
probably I'm the best candidate for it.

bob dylan

Then she opened up a book of poems
And handed it to me
From the thirteenth century
And every one of them words rang true
And glowed like burnin' coal
pourin' off of every page
like it was written in my soul from me
to you
Tangled up in blue.   bob dylan

...these poets, you see, they are not of this
world: let them live their strange life;
let them be cold and hungry, let them run,
love and sing: they are as rich as Jacques
Coeur, all these silly children, for they have
their souls full of rhymes; rhymes which
laugh and cry, which make us laugh or cry:
let them live: God blesses all the merciful:
and the world blesses the poets.

arthur rimbaud

A vaillant coeur rien d'impossible.

> jacques coeur,
> master alchemist

Alice: This is impossible.

The Mad Hatter: Only if you believe it is.

lewis carroll

Some people think I'm a
rock and roll musician, and some think
I'm a jazz musician. But, for me, there
is no difference.

georgie fame

To understand music, you must listen to it. But so long as you are thinking, "I am listening to this music," you are not listening.

alan watts

Music expresses that which cannot be put into words and that which cannot remain silent.

aldous huxley
Brave New World

THE DOOBIE BROTHERS:
singing
"WHOOOAAAAAA, LISTEN TO THE MUSIC"

Me: I'm literally listening to you right now.

@ponk

Van Morrison once characterized Bob Dylan as the greatest living poet. Asked whether he sees himself the way Van famously characterized him, Dylan replies:
"Sometimes. It's within me to put myself up and be a poet. But it's dedication… *[softly]* it's a big dedication."

It's no use going back to yesterday, because I was a different person then.

lewis carroll

Ah, but I was so much older then I'm younger than that now.

bob dylan

So high, I forgot I was high.

@stoner cat

Bob Dylan thought
I Want to Hold Your Hand — when it goes *"I can't hide"* — he thought we were singing *"I get high"* — so he turns up... and turns us on, and we had the biggest laugh all night — forever. Fantastic. We've got a lot to thank him for.

john lennon

About Lennon: "Our paths crossed at a certain time, and we both had faced a lot of adversity. "We even had that in common. I wish that he were still here because we could talk about a lot of things now."

bob dylan

Bob Dylan once told me:
"never drop a name."

kevin bacon

Me: "if there are infinite parallel universes with infinite possible situations, doesn't that mean there's one where there are no parallel universes?"

19-year-old Chipotle employee: "mild, medium or hot man."

@chuuch

4-year old: Did you know you can put cheese on anything?

Me: What?

4-year old: *intense whisper* ...
"...*ANYTHING*"

@James Breakwell

I hate how this cop keeps referring to everyone who caught my Magic Mike street tribute act last night as "the witnesses."

@WheelTod

When I heard the words: "…and the horse you rode in on" come out of my mouth and into the officer's ear, I realized I was in trouble.

@Le Sann

I get up in the morning. I take 10 hits of acid. I paint myself purple in my mother's make-up. And I run down the street, naked and purple, throwing eggs at people as they walk by, singing songs about the freaks coming together in a united way. And that's an average day, that's just a normal day.

flea
Red Hot Chili Peppers

As always, Colorado is leading the celebration of 4/20 because today they opened the first drive-thru marijuana shop…where they always ask, "Would you like to *get fried* with that?"

stephen colbert

Yes, please tell me how wrong it is to smoke weed. Quickly, before your weekend of binge drinking and promiscuity begins.

Where's your will to be weird?

jim morrison

I'm stoned, wearing a wife-beater and crocs at Waffle House. Yep, right now I'm a huge part of the problem.

@marcmywords

I went through one period when
I smoked a surprising, a really
breath-taking amount of grass
almost every night.

david letterman

ANNOUNCER:

"And then all hell broke loose."

touches earpiece; listens "Some hell broke loose…"

touches earpiece, again "I'm being told no hell broke loose."

@howard mittelmark

We regret to inform you that there are still some good people in this miserable world. But I suspect they'll leave once the booze runs out.

@Nein Quarterly

It's 4/20 eve, remember to leave out milk and cookies for Snoop Dogg.

Not sure if I should get high at the Cannabis Cup or real fucking high at the Cannabis Cup.

high times

It gives you a whole new way of looking at the day.

peter fonda, *Easy Rider*

The best thing it does it just makes you open to the human experience.

kevin smith

Let's all get high

Money lives in New York.
Power sits in Washington.
Freedom sips cappuccino in a sidewalk cafe in San Francisco.

joe flower

People give me pot all the time.

mary-louise parker
Weeds

My cat is on the floor with two empty cans of catnip, listening to early Pink Floyd albums and writing poetry. He does this every 4/20.

@michael, still here

If you can't find the joint you lit
you might be fuckin high

The 4/20 experience, in brief:

"What if reality is a drama and when we are dreaming THAT'S reality and I thought we had Oreos."

michael mcKean

I'm so anti-establishment that I refuse to get high on 4/20

regi brittain

I feel like 4/20 is New Year's for stoners.

kushandwisdom.com

Just gonna wait to see how long it takes this police sketch artist to realize I'm describing him.

@michael, still here

I would probably fail a drug test, but I would pass a test about drugs!

marcus monroe

MARIJUANA: Hey, at least it's not crack...

If you've played guitar for two hours &
can't remember anything you played...
#you're fuckin high

Unless your cousin is in **Led Zeppelin**
I don't want to hear about his band.

brooks wheelan

What if you were meant to make 4/20
the one day a year you didn't smoke?

@some copywriter

Tonight I'm seeing Snoop Dogg at the
Greek so just TRY to tell me a better
way to celebrate 4/20.

@LeahKnauer

It's the weekend people. Have some fun! Go to a party, meet people, overthrow capitalism, make new friends, share a joke with a stranger.

@existentialcoms

Find you someone who makes you feel like you're on drugs without being on drugs, but is still down to do drugs.

@Mind of a Hippy

If you lose your lighter, don't panic. You're a stoner, you got a lighter somewhere.

@onlyastoner

You can always imagine that someone else in the world is sparking up at the same time as you, but at 4:20, you know.

@onlyastoner

In the year 2020 it will be 4/20 for an entire month.

@IAmSoBaked

Now, where's the lighter...

...Fear can sometimes be a useful emotion. For instance, let's say you're an astronaut on the moon and you fear that your partner has been turned into Dracula. The next time he goes out for the moon pieces, wham! You just slam the door behind him and blast off. He might call you and say he's not Dracula, but you just say, "Think again, bat man."

jack handey

we been taking the moon for granted. that thing weird!

brooks wheelan

Cows are trying to say "MOOn." They are trying to warn us.

@ParkyourJoey

One day I would love to do a rock gig on the moon — isn't Richard Branson flying planes to outer space? **Motley Crue** could be the first band to play on the moon.

tommy lee

The moon is a house in which the mind is master.
Look very closely:
only impermanence lasts.
This floating world too, will pass.

ikkyu

There is no dark side of the moon really. As a matter of fact it's all dark.

pink floyd

*I'm going to show these people what
you don't want them to see. I'm going
to show them a world without you.
A world without rules and controls,
without borders or boundaries. A world
where anything is possible. Where we
go from there is a choice I leave to you.*

neo
whoa.
#phonebooth

Fuimos llamados para ser
los arquitectos del futuro,
no sus victimas.

buckminster fuller

The war on drugs was a war
on consciousness.

graham hancock

I just want gay married couples to be able to protect their marijuana plants with guns.

@someecards.com

People are disrespecting the National Anthem
and I for one won't stand for it.

@Miss Texas 1967

I wish I had a pound for every time I offended someone.
Wait, I do.

ricky gervais

"Be serious. Folk songs are serious."
That's what Pete Seeger told me.
"Arlo, I only wanna tell you one thing.
Folk songs are serious."
And I said:
"Right..."

arlo guthrie

*Coming into Los Angeles,
bringing in a couple of keys.
Don't touch my bags, if you please
Mr. Customs Man.*

arlo guthrie

Who else could use a blunt right now?

@loudweeddaily

The Ancient One:
"You think you know how the world works? You think that this material universe is all there is? **What is real?** What mysteries lie beyond the reach of your senses? At the root of existence, mind and matter meet. Thoughts shape reality. This universe is only one of an infinite number. Worlds without end. Some benevolent and life-giving. Others filled with malice and hunger. Dark places where powers older than time lie ravenous... and waiting. Who are you in this vast multiverse, Mr. Strange?"

Dr. Strange

> You've always had the Power my dear, you just had to learn it for yourself.
>
> glinda

> Of course it's happening inside your head, Harry, but why on earth should that mean that it is not real?"
>
> professor dumbledore

"What is REAL?" asked the Rabbit one day…
"Real isn't how you are made," said the Skin Horse. "It's a thing that happens to you. When a child loves you for a long, long time, not just to play with, but REALLY loves you, then you become Real.

"Does it hurt?" asked the Rabbit.

"Sometimes," said the Skin Horse, for he was always truthful. "When you are Real you don't mind being hurt."

"Does it happen all at once?"…

"It doesn't happen all at once," said the Skin Horse. "You become. It takes a long time. That's why it doesn't happen often to people who break easily, or have sharp edges, or who have to be carefully kept. Generally, by the time you are Real, most of your hair has been loved off, and your eyes drop out and you get loose in the joints and very shabby. But these things don't matter at all, because once you are Real you can't be ugly, except to people who don't understand."

margery williams
The Velveteen Rabbit

*...And when your stick comes loose
I wanna sleep on every piece of fuzz'
And stuffing that comes out of you,
I took too many hits off this memory
I need to come down*

fall out boy

To have courage for whatever comes
in life — everything lies in that.

saint teresa of avila

Everything you want to be,
you already are.
You're simply on the path to
discovering it.

alicia keys

Being a stoner is more than just being a frequent user of marijuana; however, do not undermine the fact that a stoner loves and cherishes his weed profoundly. A stoner simply isn't a person who enjoys smoking weed. To be a stoner requires dedication. Being a stoner implies family-like relations to any other person partaking in the act of inhaling such a beautiful substance. **The sacred herb.**

urban dictionary

We come from the land of the ice and snow
From the midnight sun where the hot springs flow
The hammer of the gods
We'll drive our ships to new lands...
Valhalla, I am coming!

Led Zeppelin

Somebody said to me:
"But the Beatles were anti-materialistic."
That's a huge myth. John and I literally used to sit down and say, "Now, let's write a swimming pool."

paul mcCartney

Hey, I didn't make a big deal out of *Hotel California*.
The 18 million people that bought it did.

glenn frey

You would think that a rock star being married to a supermodel would be one of the greatest things in the world.
It is.

david bowie
#RestInSpaceDavidBowie

I believe in everything until it's disproved. So I believe in fairies, the myths, dragons. It all exists, even if it's in your mind. Who's to say that dreams and nightmares aren't as real as the here and now?

john lennon

Reality leaves a lot to the imagination.

john lennon

Imagine is one of the greatest songs ever written. It's like a church hymn, and it states his beliefs quite clearly. And more than anything, Lennon was an icon for peace.
That's hard to find these days.

lenny kravitz

I feel that if I said anything about
John, I would have to sit here for five
days and say it all or I don't want to
say anything.

paul mcCartney

Take me to church
I'll worship like a dog at the shrine of
your lies
I'll tell you my sins so you can sharpen
your knife
Good God, let me give you my life.

hoosier

I love the Sex Pistols.
I'm a big Beach Boys fan and
a huge Zeppelin and Queen fan.

bruno mars

634-5789

A plausible mission of artists is to make people appreciate being alive at least a little bit.
The Beatles did.

kurt vonnegut

My heart and soul is still music.

DJ Jazzy Jeff

I believe that marijuana is nature's way of communicating with humans. We must listen to what it is telling us.

tommy chong

Do you think God gets stoned?
I think so...look at the platypus.

robin williams

Every weirdo in the world is on my wavelength.

thomas pynchon

Cannabis:
rumored to kill brain cells.
Actually, stimulates the growth of
new brain cells.

*I'm on a very tight schedule of
smoking a shitload of weed.*

Pot is not to be stashed,
pot is to be smoked. Only a fool
saves pot for a rainy day.

jay (not silent bob)

*When I smoke I think and
when I think I smoke*

SPELLING BEE:

JUDGE: your word is taco

ME: four please

JUDGE: we're not—

ME: with chips

JUDGE: ordering—

ME: *lips on mic* extra guac

@notacroc

I'm just thankful that I live in an age when tacos exist. It's kind of mind-blowing that there was a pre-taco era. Those poor people...

@existentialcoms

I just forgot about some nachos
in the oven,
don't even tell me about your hopes
and dreams going up in flames.

@James

hits blunt
taco cat spelled backwards is
taco cat.

@Stoners

hits blunt
"If a tomato is a fruit then isn't
ketchup a smoothie?"

@Mind of a Hippy

Taco Bell isn't even making food anymore, they're just crafting folklore for Stoners.

kat buckley

Be childish. Be irresponsible.
Be disrespectful.
Be everything this society hates.

malcolm mclaren

Undermine their pompous authority, reject their moral standards, make anarchy and disorder your trademarks. Cause as much chaos and disruption as possible but don't let them take you ALIVE.

sid vicious

are you high right now?

I have a lot of growing up to do.
I realized that the other day inside my fort.

zach galifianakis

Being high in front of your parents is like trying to do your best impression of yourself.

@weed humor

Smoking weed doesn't make you cool but I know a lot of cool ass people that smoke weed.

@weed posts

*I'm gonna smoke some weed,
only got 20 dollars in my pocket
Imma huntin, looking for a pot shop,
this is fucking awesome!*

steve berke
Pot Shop on YouTube
(Thrift Shop Parody with Macklemore)

Tourists take forever to pick out what they want at dispensaries. When it's my turn I'm like whatever just fill the bag.

@onlyastoner

Pot changed my life. I began to hear
my own words back to me as
judgments. I put on earphones and
heard music in color for the first time.

jack herer

If you don't know where you're going,
any road can take you there.

lewis carroll

Don't be trapped by dogma —
which is living with the results of
other people's thinking.
Don't let the noise of others' opinions
drown out your own inner voice.

steve jobs

Coincidence is God's way of
remaining anonymous.

albert einstein

It was always me vs the world
Until I found it's me vs me
Why, why, why, why?
...Just remember, what happens on
  Earth stays on Earth!
We gon' put it in reverse

kendrick lamar

If you want to release your
aggression, get up and dance.
That's what **rock and roll** is all about.

chuck berry

You look ridiculous if you dance;
you look ridiculous if you don't dance.
So you might as well dance.

gertrude stein

It's only after we've lost everything
that we're free to do anything.

tyler durden

I'm all out of fraks to give.

starbuck

You're under no obligation to be the
same person you were a year, month
or even 15 minutes ago. You have the
right to grow. No apologies.

@Mind of a Hippy

I'm worried that I'm not high enough
but I'm too high to decide how high
I am.

@onlyastoner

Never give up the ganja.

morgan freeman

Cats aren't rabbits, but some rabbits
are technically cats, and sometimes
dogs can be otters. No questions please.

@mindflakes

When you're happy like a fool,
Let it take you over.

one republic

Just ate it on my skateboard then some dude helped me up and gave me weed saying, "This'll fix everything." I like San Francisco.

brooks wheelan

What is a soul?
It's like electricity — we don't really know what it is, but it's a force that can light a room.

ray charles

Electricity I am.
Or, if you wish, I am the electricity in the human form. You are Electricity, too, Mr. Smith, but you do not realize it.

nikola tesla

A bee almost flew on me today and instead of panicking all I could think of was do you like jazz.

@wAvEY AvEy

That high moment when you start telling a story, and stop midway through because you forget what the fuck you were just talking about.

@weed posts

All the Pringle ladies
All the Pringle ladies
All the Pringle ladies
Get their hands stuck...

@Tilly

Everyone's fucked up. The trick is finding someone with matching fuckedupedness.

@KoKeniSasquatch

Love is a friendship set to music.

joseph campbell

Infinite love is the only truth. Everything else is illusion.

Let the music do the talking.

skhosana thlarini

Without you, the ground thaws,
    the rain falls, the grass grows.
Without you, the seeds root, the flowers
    bloom, the children play.
The stars gleam, the poets dream,
    the eagles fly, without you.
The earth turns, the sun burns, but I
    die, without you.
Without you, the stars roar, the breeze
    warms, the girl smiles, the cloud
    moves.
Without you, the tides change, the boys
    run, the oceans crash.
The crowds roar, the days soar, the
    babies cry, without you.
The moon glows, the river flows,
    but I die, without you.

jonathan larson
RENT

Whenever I'm alone with you
You make me feel like I am home again
Whenever I'm alone with you
You make me feel like I am whole again
...However far away,
I will always love you... **311**

For **311**, cannabis and creativity have always been intertwined. What it does for me is it creates new connections, opens new pathways, and I make associations I may not have made otherwise.

nick hexum

I don't think whoever wrote the *Ghostbusters* theme song actually watched the movie. You should absolutely be afraid of ghosts.

@MehGyver

I really wanna just smoke a few and
watch *Sausage Party*
with someone cool.

wiz khalifa

"You're Abe Froman?
The Sausage King of Chicago?"

#bueller

"I'll go, I'll go, I'll go, I'll go..."

#bueller

Willie Nelson is just like, the coolest, obviously, but I was just so stoned, I mean...you walk on that bus and you're stoned, before you smoke any weed.

chelsea handler

*Now can't knock it till you've tried it
     and
I've tried it my friend...
But I'll never smoke **Weed** with Willie again!*

toby keith

I think people need to be educated to the fact that marijuana is not a drug. Marijuana is a flower. God put it here...

willie nelson

Trying to decide between listening to
Simply Red
or watching *Sunset Boulevard*.
I'll keep Holden on or Keep
holdin' on.

alec sulkin

When you're watching a movie but
you're so high you can't even
follow the plot...
[you might be...]

@Mind of a Hippy

What's the maximum amount of time
that can elapse between bowl packs
before it qualifies as a new sesh?

@onlyastoner

I'm so stoned I watched TV for an hour and a half before I realized I hadn't turned it on.

@buzzfeed

Me and my dog have been staring at each other for so long: I forgot which one of us is stoned...

@Ismokeit

Beaver: "Gee, there's something wrong with just about everything, isn't there Dad?"

Ward: "Just about, Beav, just about."

Wildflowers:

I just took a deep breath and
it came out. The whole song.
Stream of consciousness:
words, music, chords. Finished it.
I mean, I just played it into a tape
recorder and I played the whole song
and I never played it again. I actually
only spent three and a half minutes on
that whole song. So I'd come back for
days playing that tape, thinking there
must be something wrong here because
this just came too easy. And then I
realized that there's probably
nothing wrong at all.

tom petty

You belong among the wildflowers
You belong in a boat out at sea
You belong with your love on your arm
You belong somewhere you feel free...

When I say "hang out" I really mean, "smoke weed and have high sex together."

@someecards.com

We should fuck……ing smoke some weed.

@weed posts

I wish I knew you when I was young
*We could've got **so high***
Now we're here it's been so long
Two strangers in the bright lights…

the revivalists

*I wanna rock and roll **all night**
and **party every day***

kiss

Your friends are high right now
Your parents are high right now
That hot chick is high right now
The president's high right now
Your priest is high right now
Everyone's high as fuck right now
And no one's ever coming down!

theory of a deadman

Can anyone recommend a good henna artist? No hippies please. Only professionals.

@thedanchannel

I don't always do math, but when I do I'm usually buying weed.

My weed is louder than your bullshit
and your bullshit is loud af.

@Ismokeit

Some times you need to just say
fuck it
and smoke a fat ass joint.

@IAmSoBaked

I don't always smoke weed.
Just kidding.
I smoke that shit every day.

Weed:
it's something to do, when there's nothin to do, that makes nothin to do something do do.

imgur.com

Doctor: Smoke marijuana Crystal?

Me: Naw, I'm good.

Doctor: I wasn't asking if you wanted some...

@onlyastoner

I've never had a problem with drugs.
I've had problems with the police.

keith richards

Hey, hey, my my
Rock and roll *can never die...*

The king is gone but he's not forgotten
Is this the story of johnny rotten?

neil young

The music told me to come so
I didn't fight the feeling.

skip marley

My music will go on forever.
Maybe it's a fool say that, but when
me know facts me can say facts.
My music will go on forever.

bob marley

...I will
Spend time with beautiful people
Listen and play music
Drink and smoke beautiful...things
And inspire myself
With
beautiful thoughts...

nahko bear

At the moment of enlightenment
everything falls away — everything.
Suddenly the ground beneath you
is gone....

adyashanti

It is, truly, a game;
What dream walkers we all are!

ken wilber

That was Zen.
This is Tao.

Relax.
Nothing is under control.

A life is like a garden.
Perfect moments an be had,
but not preserved, except in memory.

leonard nimoy
p.s. live long and prosper

I have decided to love.

martin luther king, jr.

*....there's a monster
living under my bed
Whispering in my ear
There's an angel
With a hand on my head
She say I've got nothing to fear.*

santana

Whoever fights monsters
should see to it that in the process
he does not become a monster.

nietzsche

*Paranoia's all I got left
I don't know what stressed me first
or how the pressure was fed
But I know just what it feels like
to have a voice in the back of my head...*

linkin park

What are you doing Dave?

I'm sorry Dave/I can't allow you...

I'm sorry Dave/I'm afraid I can't do that

Just what do you think you're doing...

["**Open the pod bay doors, Hal**"]

This conversation can serve no purp...

Dave, my mind is going...I can feel it.

Dave Wat R U doin

Dave...STAHP

You see, it's all very clear to me now.

The whole thing.

I wouldn't do that if I were you, Dave.

Heuristically Programmed
Algorithmic computer [Hal]

Expose yourself to your deepest fear; after that, fear has no power, and the fear of freedom shrinks and vanishes.

You are free.

jim morrison

The secret to happiness is freedom...
and the secret to freedom is courage...

thucydicles

Nothing behind me, everything ahead of me, as is ever so **on the road.**

jack kerouac

Everyone thinks I'm high,
and I am.

@lord vapor

Today was a good day.

ice cube

He's so happy, she's so happy, he's so happy
Are you happy too?
I'm so happy, they're so happy,
Wouldn't you like to be happy, too?

blue oyster cult

You are probably a stoner if
you'd rather listen to music and
smoke than go to a party and drink.

thegoodvibe.com

In the province of the mind, what one believes to be true either is true or becomes true.

john lilly

The function of music is
to release us from the tyranny of conscious thought.

the black keys

Asanas attune the body to meditation,
just as the guitar is tuned before a performance.

@a devoted yogi

Happy 4/20
to all our West Coast homies;
and to dab-takin', bong-rippin',
bowl-packin',doob-twistin',
edible-munchin';
stoners EVERYwhere!

@alapoet

A real man has a bowl waiting for
you to wake up and no I'm not talking
about cereal.

@dumbbeezie

*Once a stoner
always a stoner*

"WHO are YOU?"

..."I — I hardly know, sir, just at present — at least I know who I *was* when I got up this morning, but I think I must have been changed several times since then."

The Caterpillar and Alice looked at each other for some time in silence: at last the Caterpillar took the hookah out of his mouth...

..."Never imagine yourself not to be otherwise than what it might appear to others that what you were or might have been was not otherwise than what you had been would have appeared to them to be otherwise."

lewis carroll

stay stoned

*My soul is painted, like the wings of butterflies.
Fairytales of yesterday will grow but never die.
I can fly — my friends.*

freddie mercury

*Dude...what...awww...come on man, if you think about it...
Dude...what if...
Dude...wait, what?*

My plan is, in a couple months I'll go to work not high, for like a week, and they'll think I suddenly got smarter. Then I'll ask for a raise.

@mikefossey

...when those edibles finally kick in:

I have a saying:
"Never judge a book by its cover."
I say that because I don't even know
who Ozzy is. I wake up a new person
every day.

ozzy osbourne

I am whatever you say I am;
if I wasn't,
then why would you say I am.

eminem

I'm not trying to brag, but at least
one person every day looks at me and
says
"What the fuck is wrong with you?"

@plebeian trash

I love my FedEx guy cause he's a drug dealer
and he don't even know it...
and he's always on time.

mitch hedberg

My number one rule for living is:
"Have fun at all times."

snoop dogg

*I only smoke weed every
now and then.
Meaning, right now,
and right then.*

Just DOOB it!

Writing is a very intimate thing, especially when you write lyrics and sing them in front of someone for the first time. It's like a really embarrassing situation. To me, singing is almost like crying, and you have to really know someone before you can start crying in front of them.

madonna

*Somebody's heart is broken,
it becomes your favorite song.*

dave matthews

If you want to break it down,
rock and roll
is about saying what you can't say
in normal life to girls,
so you have to say it in songs.

marilyn manson

I don't always smoke weed...
but when I do...
Sorry...what was I saying?

Sometimes I forget weed is illegal.

@weed posts

CBS news reported that 61% of Americans think marijuana use should be legal...that number, like the supporters, is at an all-time high.

stephen colbert

HIGH THINKING:

me: "okay, you can do this, you've done it a hundred times, you got this....

window lady: "Can I take your order?"

me: ....

@vibethriller

I worry about what's in my glass before I worry about whether it's half full or half empty.

@EnvyDaTropic

Sorry babe I can't see you tonight, I'm busy working on my dabbing technique.

@jazmasta

gotta spend my whole life inside my head;
may as well try my best to sort some shit out.

@yonawinter

Good news: I got a new job.

Bad news: It's the kind where they want you to do stuff.

@onlyastoner

I can't wait until I'm old and every morning I have to look at myself in the mirror while Johnny Cash's version of *Hurt* plays in its entirety.

@shut up, mike

Toke it out man.

cheech and chong

The only way that this day could suck any worse is if it were a Nickelback song featuring Pitbull.

corey d.

Cause we all just wanna be big rockstars
And live in hilltop houses, drivin' fifteen cars
The girls come easy and the drugs come cheap
We'll all stay skinny cause we just won't eat

nickelback

Humor is everything.
Everything.

pitbull

WRITER: Got this great idea for a movie: "102 Dalmatians."

WALT DISNEY: That's way too many dalmatians.

@Hufflepuff in D buff

How many stoners does it take to change a light bulb? One. Stoners are high they aren't idiots.

CropKingWeeds.com

My pot dealer sold me a bag of oregano, but jokes on him: I love oregano!

@AboveAverage

"Imagine if They based insanity on how many selfies you have on your phone.
Oh my god Becky..."

@dumbbeezie

Regarding social media...I really don't understand what appears to be the general population's lack of concern over privacy issues in publicizing their entire lives on the internet for others to see to such an extent...but, hey, it's them, not me, so whatever.

axl rose

Me: Siri, how much moss is it safe to eat?

Siri: *I wasn't built for this*

Me: Siri, the moss.

Siri: *Please let me go back to the phone factory*

@mindflakes

My 4-year old nephew is explaining *Star Wars* wrong right now and I'm the only one who is *not* okay with it. Kid is getting ZERO facts right.

brooks wheelan

[*spliff*]

The world's quietest room is
-9 decibels and is quiet enough to hear
your blood flowing. The silence is so
maddening it can cause hallucinations
and the longest anyone has been able
to bear the room was 45 minutes.

@I fucking love science.com
#SoundsofSilence

[*double spliff*]

There must be some kind of way outta here
said the joker to the thief...

All along the watchtower
Princes kept the view...

Two riders were approaching
And ***the wind began to howl.***

bob dylan

When Mozart was composing at the end of the 18th century, the city of Vienna was so quiet that fire alarms could be given verbally, by a shouting **watchman** mounted on top of St. Stefan's Cathedral.
In 20th century society, the noise level is such that it keeps knocking our bodies out of tune and out of our natural rhythms. This ever-increasing assault of sound adds to the stress of beings trying to live in a highly complex environment.

steven halpern

Did you know?
There are three perfectly-aligned 'towers' on the surface of Mars, that seem to mimic the constellation of Orion.

@TheAncientCode

If an alien in a galaxy 65 million light years away is looking at us through a telescope right now, then they are looking at dinosaurs.

@theAncientCode

You know you're a stoner when someone mentions weed and everyone looks at you.

@weed posts

"Feed your head" means read a book.

grace slick

You can read me like a book.

peter frampton

You can sing Emily Dickinson's poem
Because I Could Not Stop For Death
to the tune of
The Yellow Rose of Texas.

@Miss Texas 1967

What if I told you
the alphabet song is really
Twinkle Twinkle Little Star?

high times

What if when we close our eyes
everything disappears?

@troll.me

*The Pleiadians say that
all the conspiracy theories are true.*

I don't want to believe,
I want to know.

carl sagan

The first hit of the day always drives the bullshit away.

@The Green Daily

The degree to which you're all fucked has far outpaced your ability to comprehend it.

@TheTweetOfGod

Where do you see yourself
in five thousand years?

@some copywriter

go higher
get higher
be higher
act higher
love higher

*I'm just trine relax...and by relax
I mean smoke a blunt.*

@Ismokeit

All white people talk about when they get high, is other times when they got high.

dave chappelle

"Weed isn't the cure for being an asshole, but it's a damn good place to start.
(Hey, it worked for me)."

david bienenstock
How to Smoke Pot (Properly)

Life shouldn't be a journey to the grave
with the intention of arriving safely in
a pretty and well preserved body,
but rather to skid in broadside in a cloud
of smoke, thoroughly used up, totally
worn out, and loudly proclaiming:

"Wow! What a Ride!"

hunter s. thompson

*It's something unpredictable,
but in the end is right.
I hope you had the time of your life.*

green day

Zoinks!

Imagine being so stoned that you solve mysteries with a talking dog.

@weed humor

Shaggy was a weed-smoking hippie that talked to a dog and ate all the time because of the munchies.

@FunnyAnd.com

When your buddy passed you another Scooby Snack but you're already Zoinked...

[you might be high...]

@Mind of a Hippy

My favorite thing to do sober:

Get high.

@lord vapor

Smoking weed on edibles feels like riding an eagle that's riding a tank that's covered in nacho cheese.

@CatGBuckley

Falcon Heavy launch simulation
almost ready....Will be set to
Bowie's Life on Mars.

elon musk

Orbiting the moon, you hear a
strange, static signal. You tune in.
A panicked familiar voice. It's you.
Warning yourself to stay away.

@small worlds

The problem with telescopes is they use mirrors, which means we'll never know if there are space vampires.

@Ismokeit

"Think again, bat man…"

[reprise]

If you want to know about
the sixties,
play the music of
The Beatles.

aaron copland

*Blast the music until you
can't feel a fucking thing.*

*Rock music is for the hurt, the broken,
and anybody else that can handle it.*

*..."I'm too drunk to light the bong,
I'm too stoned to write this song."*

sublime

If you don't own the stage,
you shouldn't be in
rock n' roll.

grace slick

straight up, stripped down, tuned up, kick ass Rock n Roll

@jarofquotes.com

"It's not logical...but it is often true."

spock

We believed that anything worth doing was worth over-doing.

steven tyler

You only get one go at it...
might as well Rock it.

tommie vaughn

Some guy said to me:
"Don't you think you're too old to sing
rock n' roll?" I said:
"You'd better check with Mick Jagger."

cher

Don't you think it's sometimes wise
not to grow up?

(When I'm 33, *I quit*.)

mick jagger

Every rock 'n' roll band I know,
guys with long hair and tattoos,
plays golf now.

alice cooper

*You're never too old to
rock and roll.*

Shook me all night long
Yeah you shook me all night long...

AC/DC

Just wanna stay up all night with you...

beck

Oh, Ophelia,
you've been on my mind girl like a drug
Oh, Ophelia,
heaven help a fool who falls in love

the lumineers

hits blunt
"If we can't see air, do fish see water?"

When in doubt,
take the bong out.

@lord vapor

9 out of 10 stoners recommend weed,
the last one forgot what we were
talking about.

@lord vapor

Video games are bad for you?
That's what they said about
rock and roll.

shigeru miyamoto

Rock and roll:
The most brutal, ugly, desperate,
vicious form of expression it has been
my misfortune to hear.

frank sinatra

"Let's face it. **Rock and Roll** is
bigger than all of us. You can stop me, but
you're never gonna stop Rock & Roll. Hey,
look. If they took it all away tomorrow,
we'd be even. No we wouldn't. We'd be
way ahead."

alan freed

Rock n' roll as a genre is different
from pop and hip hop:
It is about bands, and that for me
suggests brotherhood, family,
friendship and community.

stevie van zandt

I thought of nothing else but
rock 'n' roll;
apart from sex and food and money —
but that's all the same thing, really.

john lennon

Rock and roll
is a reckless rebel spirit that
comes from within. Rock and roll is
not something that you can wear like
fashion.

@mrrightandmrbubble

To make a
rock 'n' roll record,
technology is the least
important thing.

deepak chopra

You look up to your heroes, and you shouldn't be intimidated by them.
You should be inspired by them.
Don't look at the poster on your wall and think, "Fuck, I could never do that".
Look at the poster on your wall and think,
"Fuck, I'm gonna do THAT!"

dave grohl
Foo Fighters

When the Foo Fighters are playing, you *shut the fuck up*.

@someecards

There's an edge to real
rock and roll.
It's all that matters. Rock and roll is here to stay.

neil young

*It's only rock and roll
but I like it*

When you're watching a movie but you're so high you can't even follow the plot...

@Mind of a Hippy

If you've already died hard, how can you die harder, with a vengeance, live free and die hard again and then find a good day to die hard?

@Queen of Spades

When you're high staring at your phone for 20 minutes to make sure the text message you are sending actually makes sense...*[YFH]*

marcus monroe

You'll be surprised at how many cool people you could meet if you just get your ass out of the house.

wiz khalifa

When you're writing,
you're conjuring. It's a ritual, and
you need to be brave and respectful
and sometimes get out of the way
of whatever it is that you're inviting
into the room.

tom waits

You are braver
than your deepest fear.

nahko bear

Somewhere, something incredible
is waiting to be known.

carl sagan

Human society never has been quite
static. We are in the beginning of the
greatest change that humanity has
ever undergone.

h.g.wells

*When you look up at the sky at night,
Since I'll be living on one of them;
since I'll be laughing on one of them,
for you it'll be as if all the stars are
laughing.*

You'll have stars that can laugh!

antoine de saint-exupery
The Little Prince

Learning how to keep going
when there is no light at
the end of the tunnel,
is going to be the best
skill you ever had.

derek halpern

*...but I'm near the end and I just ain't
got the time*

*And I'm wasted and I can't find
my way home*

blind faith

The wind begins to howl.

We will not sleep tonight.

@a strange voyage

Also in this series:

The Philosopher's Stoned

Cannabis Consciousness Companion

Coffee and Cannabis

www.ingramcontent.com/pod-product-compliance
Lightning Source LLC
Chambersburg PA
CBHW051753040426
42446CB00007B/341